Burgundy Travel Guide

Sightseeing, Hotel, Restaurant & Shopping Highlights

Pamela Harris

Table of Contents

Burgundy

Burgundy is a hilly area of eastern France that is known for its diverse selection of wines. The region starts just south of Dijon with the Côte d'Or, which in itself is divided into two separate areas; Côte de Nuits to the north and Côte de Beaune to the South. The northern part is named after the town of Nuits-St-Georges and is renowned for its red wines. Joined to the Côte d'Or is Côte Chalonnaise, Mâconnais and Beaujolais. The area of Chablis sits on its own to the west.

60,000 acres of land are in use for wine production from which comes some 200 million bottles of wine. This is split into one-third red wine and two-thirds white wine. I am sure most of us are familiar with bottles of Beaune (medium-body red wine) and Chablis (dry white wine) but you should also try the Corton and Pommard (full-bodied reds). Two grapes are primarily used for wine production in Burgundy; Chardonnay (white) and Pinot Noir (red). Other grapes in use are: Gamay (Beaujolais), St-Bris (Sauvignon Blanc) and Bouzeron (Aligoté).

Wines are classified into the appellation system which includes the Grand Cru and the Premier Cru along with village wines and sub-village wines. There are approximately 40 Grand Cru vineyards in Chablis and the Côte d'Or. While the sub-village appellations are at the bottom of the list with careful selection it is possible to find some decent wines among them.

The inheritance laws in France are in some way responsible for the confusion with wines and the amount of labels that are very similar. When the owner of a vineyard dies the estate has to pass to all the beneficiaries in equal parts, it cannot go to a sole beneficiary. This means that there are many small estates that produce wines of very different quality but with names that can be almost identical. The small estates mean small quantities and if it is a top quality wine this can lead to high prices as demand grows.

Culture

It wasn't until the late 18th century that Burgundy became part of France, before then it was reigned over by the powerful Burgundy Dukes. The history of Burgundy and wine stretches way back to Roman times when the Romans started planting grapes in the area. Tales of wine being produced in the region are in Eumenes' Discources in A.D. 312 and this appears to be the oldest written reference. In the Middle Ages the monasteries were put to good use as the monks made wine and sold it to the nearby towns and eventually to Paris.

By 1395 standards had been set for the Burgundy winemakers and in 1416 King Charles IV decided that the wine of the area was special and made clearly defined boundaries for the region. Agreements between traders meant that the wines of Burgundy could be enjoyed by other countries and supplies were sent by boat to Belgium and England. The French revolution in 1789 devastated many of the monasteries where the wine was made and the huge vineyards were divided into smaller parcels of land.

The Burgundy region has not one but five villages in **the prettiest villages of France** category as well as three World Heritage Sites and a very unique medieval building project. There are some fantastic events and festivals throughout the year to celebrate wine, history, art and life so you will be sure to find something to suit your taste.

Go along to the Parc de l'Arbre Sec in Auxerre and join in the three days of the Aux Zarbs musical mayhem. The open-air festival takes place in the middle of July every year and features singers and groups from all over France and beyond. For music lovers of a different kind there are jazz concerts the first three Fridays of August on the shores of Lake Kir. Southeast of Dijon the open air concerts of the D'Jazz à la Plage are for everyone, young and old.

For opera lovers there is the International Baroque opera festival in the town of Beaune as well as numerous other wine-related festivals in the same town. In the heart of the Puisaye to the west of Dijon is Château Saint-Fargeau. Every year there is a spectacular sound and light show with 600 actors taking part and enacting ten centuries of history in amazing and colourful pageants.

There is just so much to do and see it is hard to know where to start but the biggest theatre event in France takes place in the streets of Chalon-sur-Saône. The four day festival takes place at the end of July every year and performers come from all over Europe and beyond to take part in the Chalon dans la Rue (Chalon in the Street). Around 300,000 spectators come to witness the 1000 or so performances that take place in the streets and on stages. Puppets, clowns, acrobats and fire eaters; come and have a wander through the streets, you never know what might be waiting to surprise you round the next corner.

Pop and rock is offered at the Alésia the Nuits Péplum event and the Festival of Words at La Charité-sur-Loire lets you join and use your talking talents. Lormes is home to the Festival of French Song and folk music at the Fête de la Vielle held in Anost.

Location & Orientation

The narrow Burgundy region starts one hundred kilometres southeast of Paris and stretches 360 kilometres south towards Lyon. In this 31,500 sq. km there are an amazing 1000 kilometres of canals. The Canal of Burgundy has 209 locks for boats to pass through. Canal barges and houseboats are available to hire and are a popular way of travelling through the region. Some of the locks have helpful and friendly lockkeepers while some locks are unmanned and need a little elbow grease to get through. Many years ago goods were transported by barge and you could have your possessions shipped from the United Kingdom all the way through France to the warmer climes of the Mediterranean.

Dijon is the capital of the Burgundy region and is also the centre of distribution and communications in the area. Dijon is just over an hour and half by high-speed (TGV) train from Paris or a slightly more sedate train journey from Basel or Geneva.

There is no international airport in the Burgundy area. To fly to the south of the region it is better to use the Lyon Saint-Exupéry airport that is 68 kilometres from Mâcon or Geneva airport. The Paris airports are about 300 kilometres away. There is a small airport in Dijon that has scheduled flights to Toulouse and Bordeaux in France but not to Paris.

Road links are excellent with fast, smooth motorways going from Dijon in all directions.

Climate & When to Visit

The Burgundy climate can be kind; the summers are warm and pleasant and quite hot in July and August. Average temperature in summer is 19°C but the highest ever recorded was a staggering 38.1°C. Apart from these two months the summer night-time temperature can be cool, so be prepared with a jumper or jacket. One of the threats of the summer months is hailstorms and in 2009 a vineyard was destroyed in this way.

Autumn brings the grape harvest and for the three or so weeks the workers in the fields are bundled up to go to work early mornings and gradually peel off the layers as the hours go by and the sun comes out. Going home means wrapping up again as the chilly evenings set in.

Winter can be cold and the lowest temperature ever recorded was minus 21.3°C. The average though is about 1.6°C. The winters are usually a dry cold though, snow does fall but there is not the damp feeling in the air like in the UK.

Springtime can be nice as the cold of winter is going away with the promise of warmer days to follow. If you are lucky and get nice weather the area is wonderful as the flowers start to blossom and there are not too many people about.

For visiting in spring and autumn it can be wet, so maybe pack some long trousers and decent hiking boots, especially if you plan on doing much walking as the paths can get slippery. In winter wrap up warm, think thick gloves, furry hats and boots. If you get a chilly there is always plenty of wine to warm you up especially a nice glass of **vin chaud** (hot spiced red wine). Don't use the 1945 Mouton Rothschild or 1787 Château Lafite though!

Sightseeing Highlights

Beaune

Beaune is known as the Champs Elysées of Burgundy and is close to famous name villages known to wine-lovers such as Pommard and Gevrey-Chambertin. In the heart of the vineyards the town has much for the visitor to see in the way of heritage without even setting foot in a vineyard. Many people come to the town whether they are professionals or beginners to learn about the region and the wines that are on offer here.

The town has everything for a wonderful stay and the level of gastronomy is like the wines, from cheap and cheerful to top class; there are brasseries, bistros offering table d'hôte menus right up to Michelin star restaurants. As you stroll through the cobbled streets and gardens full of fragrant blooms you will come across mansions from a bygone age and half-timbered buildings that hide intriguing places to eat. With over a hundred restaurants there is something for everyone. Choose from jellied ham, snails or coq au vin and don't forget to try the local cheeses of Citeaux and Eoisses.

No stay in Beaune would be complete without a wine tour of some kind. Whether it is underground to the wine cellars and their hidden treasures or a journey out to a vineyard there are hundreds of ways of being introduced to wine. A lovely way to discover the countryside and pretty villages is by hiking. In and around Beaune there are 14 marked footpaths, with different lengths and degrees of difficulty, three of these footpaths pass through vineyards so why not stop off for a spot of wine tasting on the way.

Hospice de Beaune (Hôtel de Beaune)

Rue de l'Hôtel Dieu
21200 Beaune
Tel: +33 380 244 700

This delightful hotel is set in a former alms-house that was founded in 1443 for the poor and needy. A stunning example of fifteenth century architecture is the hospital building that is now a museum. Luckily now patients go to a more modern hospital. Every November an important charity wine auction is held here.

Notre Dame Collegiate Church

Place Général Leclerc
21200 Beaune
Tel: +33 380 247 795

Over the centuries various elements have been added to the original Romanesque architecture, gothic portals and a 16th century chapel and bell tower. There is a 12th century statue of the Virgin Mary as well as tapestries depicting her life.

Burgundy Wine Museum

Hôtel des Ducs de Bourgogne
Rue d'Enfer
21200 Beaune
Tel: +33 380 220 819
www.musees-bourgogne.org

You can find anything and everything to do with viticulture here in this magnificent setting. The Burgundy Dukes lived here for a few hundred years from the 13th century onwards and they have left behind a legacy of wine-related tapestries, art and tools for us all to learn from.

Dijon

Dijon is in an ideal location on the main road from Paris to Lyon. The Dukes of Burgundy lived in the province until the late 15th century and this meant that Dijon was a place with enormous wealth and power.

There are houses in the centre of the town that date from the 18th century that are still inhabited today; but hopefully they have some modern conveniences by now. The roofs of Dijon are one of the distinguishing features of the areas architecture with glazed tiles in geometric patterns and vibrant colours of green, yellow, terracotta and black. There are about 700 hectares of parks and green spaces and many, many museums that are worth a visit

There are many important fairs held in France but Dijon is home to the International and Gastronomic Fair every autumn. The fair is in the top ten of most important fairs in France and attracts 200,000 visitors and 500 exhibitors. The international flower show Florissimo is held here every three years.

We are all familiar with Dijon mustard which was invented here in 1856 when the juice of unripe grapes was substituted in the traditional mustard recipe. How many of us know that this is also where Crème de Cassis comes from. The blackcurrant liqueur is mixed with white wine to make the drink Kir.

Dijon Opera

11 Boulevard de Verdun
21000 Dijon
Tel: +33 380 488 282
www.opera-dijon.fr

Opened in June 1998 the Dijon Opera has the most beautiful acoustics in Europe and attracts major conductors and orchestras. Many productions are brought to life here, theatre, dance and performing arts. Have a look at the programme before you plan your trip, there might just be something you would like to see.

Museum of Burgundy Life

17 Rue Sainte-Anne
21000 Dijon
Tel: +33 380 488 090
www.musees-bourgogne.org

For an insight into Dijon life pay a visit to the Museum of Burgundy Life. The museum opened in 1982 and is in the cloisters of the Bernadine Monastery. The collections show possessions and costumes about Dijon daily life from the 18th century to the beginning of the 20th century.

Dijon Cathedral

6 Rue Danton
21000 Dijon
Tel: +33 380 303 933
www.cathedrale-dijon.fr/

The present Gothic cathedral was built between 1280 and 1325 and while not the most inspiring of cathedrals it is worth visiting while you are in town.

Owl's Trail (La Chouette)

If you are visiting Dijon with children, or without, take some time to follow the Owl's Trail round the town to see the sights. The trail is named after the owl on the façade of the Notre Dame church who you must stroke for good luck! The tourist office will have the English language brochure or hire an audio guide and go owl hunting.

Augustodunum Roman Theatre

Rue Maladière
71400 Autun

The town of Autun was founded for and named after the Roman emperor Augustus when Augustodunum became his headquarters. The Roman Theatre here is huge and has a capacity of 20,000. It doesn't take much imagination to hear the roar of the crowds echoing down from the past. The theatre is free to enter and visitors can wander round at their leisure.
In late August everything changes and six hundred residents of the town come together to put on a spectacular display. The Roman theatrical show goes on for several hours and is good fun even if somewhat hard to understand. Take some blankets, cushions and drinks to make a day of it with the family.

Touro Park & Zoo

Maison Blanche
Romanèche –Thorins
Tel: +33 385 355 153
www.touroparc.com/

Touro Park might not be very big but it manages to pack 800 animals from 140 species into its 12 acres. The way the zoo is arranged means you get really close to the animals, safely of course, and see how they thrive in their home from home beautifully kept surroundings. See the white tigers, elephants, giraffes, lizards, rhinos and much more.

There is also an adventure park, a small train, monorail and an old fashioned carousel dating from 1900. Once you have seen the monkeys in the zoo why not go on the **Amazon Adventure** course and see how well you can imitate them as you swing through the jungle ropes. If you fancy a splash around after a hard day in the wilderness, there is a waterpark to cool off in. There is the Beaujolais Village and Museum, two snack bars, a restaurant and picnic areas and watch out for the souvenir shop on the way out.

The park is open every day from February 15th to November 15th.Summer hours are June 1st to August 31st 9.30am to 6.30pm and in the other months the park closes one hour earlier. The amusements open at 1.30pm each day. Adult tickets cost €15.50 to €19.50 and children €13 to €16.50 depending on the time of year.

Parc de l'Auxois (Water & Animal Park)

Route Départementale 905
21350, Arnay-Sous-Vitteaux
Tel: +33 380 496 401
www.parc-auxois.fr/

Parc de l'Auxois is far more than just an animal park. The 35 hectares have all the necessary attractions to make it a really good day out but the park is also there to educate. It is very important that every generation learns about the lifestyle of the animals and how some of them are under threat from mankind. Parc de l'Auxois plays an important part in working with other European parks and conservation organisations to protect conservation areas in Madagascar, French Guiana and Asian and African countries.

If any exotic pets are confiscated by the local authorities or not wanted by their owners they will be given refuge at the park. Turtles, ostriches, parakeets, monkeys, snakes and lemurs are all examples of the animals that have been taken in here.

For amusement there is mini-golf and playgrounds or you can take a train ride through the park. Find the maze and lose yourself, or the children, in the intricate patterns. You can wander across the suspension bridge and gaze down at the shady areas of the park and see if you can spot any of the animals taking refuge from the sun. There is a swimming pool and water games through the summer months so remember to bring your swimming costume.

There are places to eat, drink and juts relax and the park is open from 10am until 7pm every day. An adult ticket is €14 and children between 3 and 12 years old pay €10.

Muséo Parc Alésia (Interactive Museum)

1, route des Trois Ormeaux BP 49
21150 Alise-Sainte-Reine
Tel: +33 380 969 623
www.alesia.com

In 52 B.C the Gallic tribes with Vercingetorix as their leader fought Julius Caesar's Roman army at Alesia. The remains of the Gallo-Roman town can be found on the top of Mont-Auxois and several thousand people lived there over the first few centuries AD. There is a superb centre here where you can see the living quarters, how they made their crafts, the theatre and basilica etc.

The Interpretation Centre uses films, models, diorama and multimedia to plunge you into battle with reproductions of the war machines. The Roman fortifications have been built to their original height and stretch for around 100 metres. You can see daily life in a Roman camp reenacted before you as the cast of players recreate the training of legionaries and show manoeuvers and battle techniques.

The terrace around the Interpretation Centre is planted with silver birches and oaks and offers a 360° view of Mont-Auxois and the hills where the army camps of the Romans were set up.

There are audio-guides available in several languages, a souvenir shop with gifts and books and a caféteria. For children there are play areas as well as fun guides so they don't get bored. There are various ticket prices depending on which part of the site you wish to visit and the opening times change throughout the year. It is probably best to check out the website or give the site a call before you visit.

Morvan Forest

The Morvan Forest is in central Burgundy and was created in 1970 to conserve the natural environment. The park covers 2,800 km ^{2} and has just about everything anyone could wish for to make for an enjoyable outdoor life. There are six reservoirs for watersports, plus rivers and streams, some fast-running and some moving so gently you can hardly see the flow. Low mountains and woodlands hide tiny villages where the pace of life is slow and relaxation is easy.

Talking of relaxation, why not stay for a day or two in Bourbon-Lancy or Saint-Honoré-les-Bains taking the natural waters' and sampling the treatments available. Once you have been revitalized the walking opportunities abound on miles of well-marked paths. Even driving is less hassle on gently winding back roads where speed is unheard of.

A lot of the area is granite with some limestone towards the edge of the park and the area gets hot summers, cold winters and lots and lots of rain on the higher ground. The highest peak is just 900 metres but snowfall in winter can be harsh.

Treats include locally produced cheeses, hams and sausages and lime and acacia honey. The timber industry years ago was there with the sole purpose of keeping Paris warm. Today the timber is cut under strict rules and is used for the fine oak barrels for the vineyards.

One of the mysterious sounds of the forest is the cry of the stags in September as they call for partners. The moaning and wailing call echoes for miles and miles and the stags share the night with humans who are waiting to hear the call of the wild with them.

Wine Tours in Burgundy

www.authentica-tours.com/

A trip to the Burgundy region would not be complete without a tour of a wine cellar or vineyard, preferably both.

A typical basic half-day tour will take three or so hours leaving in the morning or afternoon. You will visit a wine cellar full of exceptional Burgundy wines. Accompanied by a choux pastry nibbles you will get to try red and white wines. You will also visit a wine estate in Gevrey-Chambertin that can trace its history for generations and try one of the best labels that Burgundy has to offer. Admire the immaculately kept cellars and barrels and sample Pinot Noirs that owe their flavour to tradition and local soil.

Similar half-day tours can be taken but with the addition of visiting local cheese factories and learn about the art of matching the right wine to the right cheese.

A seven hour full day tour is available that includes a private visit to a family run estate in Còte de Nuits. Follow the Champs-Elysées of Burgundy from Dijon to Beaune, stroll through vineyards and taste some of the Premier and Grand Cru white and red wines. In Beaune there is time for lunch (not included) and to visit some of the historical sights of this beautiful city.

The tour guides are chosen for their knowledge of the Burgundy area and the wines. They are all bilingual (English/ French) and will patiently answer any questions you may have. The guides are an excellent source of information for other places to visit in Burgundy and can advise on the best places to eat and drink.

Burgundy Canal Boat Trips

www.european-waterways.eu/e/info/france/canal_de_bourgogne.php

The canal opened in 1833 and connected Paris to Burgundy and still is the shortest connection between the two. Although no longer used for transportation as parts of the canal are now too shallow with a draft of only 1,40 metres, it does make a wonderful cruising holiday.

The Burgundy canal might be one of the most pleasant to cruise though in France but there are some considerations to be made. The many locks will need some manual handling and if there is not a lock-keeper, are you strong enough? Reversing into a mooring space is not like parking the car, it is rather like trying to steer a reluctant elephant backwards into a small garden shed. Boats can be cramped, although beautifully fitted out, so if you are on the tall side watch your head! Having said that, messing about on the canal is a peaceful way to travel through this beautiful region and discover the many delights on offer.

Auxerre Cathedral

Place Saint-Étienne
89000 Auxerre
Tel: +33 386 522 329
www.cathedrale-auxerre.com/

Built between 1215 and 1233 this mainly Gothic cathedral is located over an 11th century crypt. Parts were still being added to the building as late as 1540 when a renaissance cupola was added to the completed tower. The cathedral is known for the massive stained glass windows and the three Gothic style doorways. The cathedral is well worth a visit to admire the carvings and mouldings and just to be in awe of the craftsmanship that went into the making of such a beautiful place.

The cathedral is only a very short distance from the river and there are pretty parks and plazas all around to wander through. There is parking right outside the door, if you are lucky, or down along the riverfront.

The cathedral opens every day at 7.30am and closes at around 5pm. The treasure and the crypt open an hour or so later. The cathedral may be closed on occasions for special functions or holidays. The price is €3 per adult for the cathedral and €2 for the crypt. Children under 12 are admitted free of charge.

Building a Castle at Guédelon

D955
89520 Treigny
Tel: +33 386 456 666
www.guedelon.fr/

For somewhere completely different take some time to visit Guédelon. While many of the chàteaus and castles in France are being restored using modern methods and technology this one is being built from scratch using traditional ways. Fifty craftsmen covering a range of trades including rope makers, blacksmiths, carpenters, woodcutters, stonemasons, quarrymen and tile makers have started to build a castle using only traditional Middle Age techniques and materials. All the necessary materials are being found on and around the site in an abandoned quarry

The brainchild of the owner of Chàteau Saint-Fargeau the project was started in 1997 and is scheduled for completion around 2020. Guédelon is open to the public and whether you are family on holiday or a professional wishing to learn about this time in history it is a pretty amazing place to see.

Imagine a construction site with no heavy machinery, no cement mixers, no drills and saws buzzing away to disturb the peace. Take a step back in time and hear the satisfying sound of stone being carved by hand as the stonemasons chip painstakingly away to make the perfect fit. There are no cranes to lift heavy materials skywards, just simple wheel and pulley systems and the size of the bellows at the forge has to be seen to be believed.

Château de Tanlay

89430 Tanlay
Tel: +33 386 757 061
www.chateaudetanlay.fr/

Château de Tanlay is beautiful and charming; there are no other words for it. The approach to the house is across a bridge over the moat and through a pair of obelisks standing guard. The moat surrounds the house apart from the one access and would have been instrumental in protecting the château from marauding intruders. The limestone walls enclose the courtyard with cylindrical towers on the four corners and the roofs are finished with typical French slate.

The 13th century foundations were built over in the 16th to 17th centuries by François de Coligny d'Andelot who inherited the ruined site from his brother. The château is still owned by the same family of the man who created the title Marquis de Tanlay in 1705. Tanlay is famous for in particular the trompe l'oeil painted gallery and the frescoes in the tower.

Visitors are welcome from April 1st to November 2nd, but not on Tuesdays. To wander the grounds only costs €3 and a guided tour of the interior to admire the beautiful artwork and furniture costs €9 for adults and €5 for children. The guided tour includes free access to the grounds. The tours begin at set times morning and afternoon.

Mustard Factory

Moutarderie Fallot
31 rue du Faubourg
Bretonnière
21200 Beaune
Tel: +33 380 221 002
www.fallot.com/

Mmmm, who doesn't like mustard on their ham sandwiches? The Mustard Mill of Fallot has been a family owned, independent Burgundy company since 1840 and it is the first museum in France to be dedicated to mustard. An interactive tour leads through a journey of the ages where you can learn about the making and history of mustard. The tour is great for beginners and will have your sense of smell tingling as you go round.

Mustard has been around a long time and some of the materials and ancient tools are displayed and along with a sound and light show reveal many of the secrets of the world of mustard. This a novel experience in Burgundy and if you wish you can practice being a mustard-maker quicker than you can say hotdog.

La Moutarderie Fallot originally made mustard grinding the mustard seeds with a grindstone and they have managed to preserve this traditional method but with the aid of modern technology can show you how the wild mustard seed becomes the condiment we all know and love.

The price of a visit is €10 per adult and €8 between 10 and 18 years old.

Château de Pierreclos

71960 Pierreclos
Macon
Tel: +33 385 357 373
www.chateaudepierreclos.com/

In the heart of the vineyards of southern Burgundy you will find the beautiful example of medieval architecture that is Château de Pierreclos. The entrance is guarded by two gatehouses, giving way to a sweeping driveway that leads to the house. The interesting tile pattern on the gatehouse roof is continued through to some parts of the main building.

The oldest parts of the château date from the 12th century and once you have entered through the pretty gateway you reach the terrace, the romantic Mâconnais vineyard and the Romanesque church. In the château make sure you visit the armoury and the spice room. The bakery and the kitchen are fascinating and will make you very glad that we live in an age of modern conveniences.

Nine centuries of history await you in this château in Burgundy. In 1989 a programme of renovation was undertaken by the Pidault family to allow the public access to share their beautiful home. Now the château provides venues for business or private events.

A visit to the château ends in the vaulted cellars with information about the wines and of course some samples of the wine they produce. There are various tours, guided or non-guided, plus wine tastings. The chàteau is in an exceptional location and once you have had your fill of history you can visit the shop and pick up a few bottle to take home to remind you of your visit.

There are several Burgundian specialties, treats and souvenirs and make sure you try the rosé and white sparkling wines or Crément de Bourgogne. There are fruit liqueurs available with exciting flavours like vine peach, morello cherry and Ratafia au marc de Bourgogne.

Tours, dates and prices are all available on the châteaus website or just give them a call to arrange the tour that suits you the most.

Recommendations for the Budget Traveller

Places to Stay

La Maison de Mireille

2, allée du Château
89800 Courgis
Tel: +33 386 414 671
www.la-maison-de-mireille.fr/

Less than 10 kilometres from the town of Chablis is the pleasant village of Courgis. Maison de Mireille is a small privately owned hotel that caters to just six guests and sits on the edge of the sleepy village. The pretty, romantically decorated rooms are well equipped with private bathrooms and comfortable beds and furniture. There is free Wifi and free parking.

The price is €50 per night for one person or €55 for two. This includes continental breakfast with locally made bread and preserves.

Comfort Hotel Beaune

58 Route de Verdun,
21200 Beaune
Tel: +33 380 241 530
www.comfortinn.com/hotel-beaune-france-FR395

The Comfort Hotel Beaune is just a short drive from the city centre and has 46 rooms all with private bathroom. Each room has flat screen TV, satellite channels, toiletries, hairdryer, a hospitality tray and microwave. The hotel has a restaurant and bar area, an outdoor pool and terrace, a laundry service, conference and business facilities, a play area and garden. There is free parking on site and free Wifi.

The price per room is around €70 per night depending on season and children under 12 stay free if sharing a room with their parents and no extra bedding is required. Breakfast is charged at €8.50 per adult and €4 for children.

Premier Class Avallon

Rn 6 - La Cerce, RN 6,
89200 Sauvigny-le-Bois
Tel: +33 892 70 72 51
www.premiereclasse.com/

The Avallon is part of the Premier Class chain and if you want budget accommodation you can't beat staying here.

The rooms are impersonal, the soundproofing is not great but for a bed for the night when driving the long road north-south or east-west it makes an affordable stopping place. More of a transit hotel than somewhere to spend a holiday as there are no frills or charm but it serves its purpose. There is Wifi, vending machines and 24 hour access with a credit card so no restriction on arrival times.

A double room in the middle of June for two people costs just €28. Beat that! It is outside of the town right opposite the three star La Relais Fleuri, so don't get them mixed up.

Hotel Kyriad

35 Place De Beaune
71100 Châlon-sur-Saône
Tel: +33 385 900 800
www.kyriad.com/

The Kyriad in Châlon-sur-Saône is in the heart of the town right by a shady tree-lined plaza. The rooms are comfortably furnished with modern décor and a nice touch is a welcome tray full of goodies when you arrive. The rooms have private bathrooms, TV, hairdryer and free Wifi. Parking is easy right outside and the river and main attractions of the town are within walking distance.

There is an unusual bar / dining room with a natural stone curved ceiling and gaily checked tablecloths. Breakfast and other meals are available in the hotel. In August a double room will cost you €60 for two people.

Hotel Quick Palace

Rue de Bruxelles - ZA des Macherins
89470 Moneteau
Tel: +33 386 534 475
www.quickpalace.com/

Super easy access to the Quick Palace Hotel off the motorways N6 and A6 make this a good choice for overnight stays while travelling. Just north of the town of Auxerre and opposite thickly wooded areas the hotel has all you need for a comfortable night's stay. The rooms are soundproofed, have private bathrooms with toiletries and TV with satellite channels.

A self-service buffet breakfast is available from 6.30am each morning with a good selection of pastries, brioches, preserves, cereals, juices and hot drinks. The breakfast is a very reasonable €5.50.

A double room can be booked for around €30 depending on the time of year. There are some good offers on the hotel website, some with breakfast included.

Places To Eat & Drink

L'Antre II Mondes

21, rue d'Ahuy
21000 Dijon
Tel : +33 380 580 208
www.antre2mondes.com

If you are a fan of rock music and love medieval times then this is the place to go in Dijon. The atmosphere is great with huge wooden tables and grey walls decorated with medieval reminders. On Friday and Saturday lunchtimes there is a traditional folk atmosphere but in the evening the music turns into rock as the friendly owners play your favourite songs. The staff are friendly, they welcome families and if you want to eat at a unique restaurant, this is definitely it.

They serve excellent snacks and sandwiches as well as an interesting selection of historical and regional dishes. Choose from salads, a varied selection of meats cooked mediaeval style and you can wash it down with a glass of mead, or a pint of Mandubienne, a traditional Dijon beer. Prices start at €5 and they are open all day, every day.

La Cassolette

466 of Route Nationale 6
Creches sur Saone 71680
lacassolette.e-monsite.com/

The pretty pastel colours and friendliness of the charming gentleman owner makes this a very worthy stopping place in the Macon area. If your French is not great he will help you in his very best English without making you feel silly. This is an excellent restaurant and there really should be more like it.

The freshly cooked dishes all use local ingredients so the menu is very regional. There is a three course daily menu which is excellent value at €14.50 which includes a starter, a warm main course and a choice of local cheeses or dessert.

Au Bureau

5 rue de Beaudelaire,
71100 Chalon-sur-Saone,
Tel: +33 385 482 801
www.aubureau-chalonsursaone.fr/

Right in the centre of the town and by the railway station Au Bureau is open all day, every day and there is always something happening. Poker nights, concerts, theme nights and all the big matches live make this a very popular place to go.

The menu is very different with many of the dishes served on slate, there are exciting meat platters, huge burgers and a good selection of other items to tempt you. The dessert section looks very good so make sure you leave some room. The daily menu is €10.

The Publican Pub

44 rue Maufoux,
21200 Beaune
Tel: +33 380 207 622

This is a good English pub/restaurant. The prices are very reasonable for food and drink and the wines they serve come from the owner's in-laws. The seating is great with lots of comfortable couches and chairs and there is a terrace for a drink in the sun. They serve platters of meats, cheese and fish and you won't leave feeling hungry. Prices start at just €3.

Les Café Des Amis

18, rue Carnot
21500 Montbard
Tel: +33 380 920 060

Cheap, friendly and colourful is the best way to describe this café. The owner decides the dishes for every day and one day it can be a delicious chicken curry, the next a big pot of stew. They always use the best seasonal produce so the menu varies throughout the year.

The main dish of the day is €7.50 or the three course daily menu is €11.50. When you have finished your meal have a game of cards with the owner, he is more than willing to sit and chat with you. The bar is open to welcome you every day of the week.

Places to Shop

Flea Market

Place des Fontaines
89600 Saint-Florentin
Tel: +33 386 351 186
www.saint-florentin-tourisme.fr

Take a wander around a French flea market or **brocante** as they are known locally. Hunt out some old, or not so old, French treasures. What could be better than a Sunday morning rummaging through old boxes searching for hidden goodies? Afterwards find a bistro and enjoy a glass of wine, Burgundy of course.

Saint-Florentin is just one of many markets. There are big ones and small ones held all over France, some only March to October and some all year round. There are also major markets at Aillant-sur-Tholon and Mézilles.

Shopping in Beaune

http://www.beaune-tourism.com/

There are 500 shops in the centre of Beaune that will cater to your every need so it is very difficult to choose just one. Half the fun of shopping in another country is wandering round window shopping and browsing, so make a day of it and then visit one of the many places to eat for a spot of lunch. Parking is easy as there are 5,000 spaces to fill in and around the area.

Many of the streets are pedestrianised, the shop windows are colourful and beautifully decorated and the shopkeepers are polite and professional and only too happy to help. Every other shop seems to sell wine or wine related articles so finding a good vintage or two shouldn't be difficult. There are a multitude of delicatessens, arts and craft shops, a wine library, clothes and shoe shops and plenty of banks to get the necessary spending money from.

Cluny, Carrots & Chocolates

Saône-et-Loire
Burgundy

Cluny has a marvellous outdoor market on a Saturday morning. There is so much locally produced food you won't know what to buy first. Cheeses made from goat's milk, organic vegetables and fruits, gingerbread, homemade pâtés and of course plenty of wine. There are also clothes, wickerwork and some furniture.

Cluny also has one of Burgundy's great chocolate producers; Germain-Au Pêché Mignon is family run and you can taste the most exquisite handmade goodies. There is very sensibly a tearoom and café for trying the delicious pastries inside the century old cake shop that the family have transformed.

Wine Shopping in Beaune

Avenue Charles de Gaulle
21200 Beaune
Tel: +33 380 240 809
www.vinscph.fr/

For the past 25 years the owners of La Grande Boutique Du Vin in Beaune have worked with local wine growers who have small or medium size vineyards. The selection of wines to choose from is vast with over 1000 different labels. The white two-storey building doesn't betray from the outside the treasures hidden within and the wooden shelves hold rows and rows of neatly displayed bottles and boxes. The staff are always ready to help and quite happy to let you taste the wines before making the all-important decision of which one, or ten, to buy.

Galeries Lafayette

41 – 49 rue de la Liberté
21000 Dijon
Tel: +33 380 448 212
www.galerieslafayette.com/

Galeries Lafayette is one of the biggest chains of stores in France and the stores are usually in magnificent old buildings that have been around for hundreds of years and Dijon is no exception. The building itself will take your breath away with the carvings and mouldings on the exterior. Mingle with the elegantly dressed French ladies as they glide through the many floors taking their time over what to buy. There is fashion, food, jewellery, perfumes, shoes and household goods to browse through. Visit the caféteria to rest your weary feet once you have shopped until you drop, or just to leave the menfolk in while you go round a second time! Opening hours are generally Monday to Saturday. 9.30 am to 7.30 pm.

Made in the USA
San Bernardino, CA
26 March 2017